African Violets
and related plants

A Wisley Handbook

African Violets
and related plants

BILL WALL

Cassell

The Royal Horticultural Society

THE ROYAL HORTICULTURAL SOCIETY

Cassell Educational Limited
Villiers House, 41/47 Strand,
London WC2N 5JE
for the Royal Horticultural Society

First published 1990
Second edition 1991

British Library Cataloguing in Publication Data

Wall, Bill.
  African violets and related plants
  1. Pot plants. African violets. Cultivation
  I. Title   II. Royal Horticultural Society
  Series
  635.9′3382

  ISBN 0-304-32008-0

Photographs by Harry Smith Collection, Dibley's
Efenechtyd Nurseries, Tony Clements, Michael Warren and Richard Gilbert
Line drawings by Graham Wall
Typeset by Chapterhouse Ltd, Formby
Printed in Hong Kong by Wing King Tong Co. Ltd

Cover: 'Delft', a gold-medal African violet with huge flowers.
p. 1: 'Silver Milestone Star' is a large-flowered hybrid African
violet.
  Photographs by Tony Clements
p. 2: florist's gloxinias, descended from Sinningia speciosa,
are popular houseplants.
Back cover: 'Pansy-flowered' Streptocarpus hybrids can
produce flowers from spring through to early winter.
  Photograph by Michael Warren

Contents

Introduction

Saintpaulias, commonly known as African violets, are members of the Gesneriaceae – a plant family which embraces well over 2,000 species of mostly tropical plants in about 125 genera, widely distributed throughout the world. The majority have showy flowers, usually of five petals, sometimes four, joined together at the base to form a tube. This may be short, as in *Saintpaulia*, or long in other genera such as *Streptocarpus*, with two larger lobes of the petals forming a lip, while the florist's gloxinia (*Sinningia speciosa*) has large, equal, symmetrical lobes to all the petals. Seed is readily produced by most species and is very fine; it is contained in a superior ovary, that is to say with all the petals and sepals below the seed capsule, and the whole floral assembly is held in a five-parted calyx, often with leaf-like pointed lobes. The leaves are basically oval or spear-shaped and are frequently coloured, strikingly so in the case of *Episcia*; they may be either hairy or smooth.

The habit of growth of gesneriads is diverse, as one might expect with such a large family. First, we have the fibrous-rooted group, which embraces *Saintpaulia*, *Streptocarpus*, *Columnea* and *Episcia*. This includes clump-forming plants and plants which form rosettes at the end of stolons, and long-stemmed types which often root along their stems. A second group produces scaly rhizomes, almost catkin-like in appearance, formed on runners of varying lengths below the soil, and is typified by *Achimenes* and *Koehleria*. Finally, there are plants which develop tubers at or below soil level, as does *Sinningia*. These, like the rhizomed species, require a drier period of dormancy, generally in the winter after flowering (see also figure 3, p. 20).

There are also a few genera of superb alpine plants, such as *Haberlea* and *Ramonda*, which are not dealt with here (see the Wisley handbook, *Alpines the easy way*, for further information). This book is concerned with gesneriads used as decorative pot plants in the house, conservatory or greenhouse.

Opposite: *Streptocarpus* 'Karen' is typical of the British hybrids developed in the 1970s

The majority of gesneriads are easily cultivated in pots or, in some cases, hanging baskets. Their main requirements are:

warm conditions, not below 55°F (13°C) in winter, although streptocarpus will accept lower temperatures;
good light, but not direct sunlight, for maximum flower production;
an open peat-based compost giving very free drainage;
and a dormant or semi-dormant period after flowering.

A few gesneriads are very difficult to grow as ordinary house-plants. Episcias are in this category, but their combination of brilliant flowers and colourful leaves may be enjoyed by growing them in a terrarium or fish-bowl type of container, preferably under lights indoors where the necessary high temperature and high humidity can be maintained.

For the purposes of this book, the family has been divided into groups requiring similar culture. Growing requirements, propagation methods and brief descriptions are given for the most readily obtainable species, hybrids and cultivars within each group. With the florist's gloxinias and African violets well established as houseplants, it is hoped that this handbook may tempt readers to try other gesneriads which may be grown in the same conditions, as well as some that present more of a challenge.

Opposite above: *Episcia cupreata* 'Silver Queen' combines beautiful foliage with showy flowers
Below: *Achimenes* 'Purple King' produces its lovely flowers throughout the summer

General cultivation

IN THE HOME

In warm, centrally heated rooms where the temperature is 65–80°F (19–26°C), African violets are the supreme flowering houseplants. They are generally bought as plants in flower in 3½ in. (9 cm) pots and taken home to provide an instant splash of colour indoors and, given the right treatment, they will go on flowering for several months. They should be placed in a light position, but not where direct sunlight can shine on them through glass, and not where they would get radiant heat from being close to a radiator or an open fire.

Plants as obtained will have their pots full of roots and will therefore need to be fed, using a high potash fertilizer at every other watering. The pot should ideally be placed on a layer of small pebbles in a dish or saucer to allow free drainage. However, I doubt very much whether it is of any benefit to keep water in the saucer to increase humidity round the plant: in fact, if the room temperature is likely to fall much below 55°F (13°C), this will heighten the possibility of fungal attack to the lower leaves of the plant. Only water the plant when the compost is virtually dry, preferably by immersing the pot in water for 15 minutes or so and allowing it to drain before replacing in its saucer. It is easy to over-water saintpaulias, particularly since the leaves of the rosette are usually so closely overlapping. As the plant continues to flower, the old flower stems should be pulled off when they become dry, and any leaves that become dried or disfigured should be removed with a sideways pressure so that they are completely detached from the main stem. Although flowering normally continues for several months, it will eventually cease, and this is the time to give the plant a somewhat cooler rest period for a month or so, to repot and to propagate it (see p. 29).

Given the same conditions of light and temperature as saintpaulias, the various species and hybrids of *Columnea* will flower very freely at their appropriate season and some have the attraction of coloured foliage. The miniature sinningias are also excellent for warm rooms, since with enough heat they do not become dormant and are truly ever-blooming. These plants, I believe, have great potential and they are being taken notice of in the USA.

African violets are available in a wide range of colours

For cooler conditions, the modern streptocarpus hybrids are becoming very popular as flowering houseplants. Like the saintpaulias, they require a light but not sunny position and need to be fed regularly with a high potash fertilizer, when they will flower continuously from April to November in a temperature range of 50–70°F (10–20°C). They are not as compact in growth as saintpaulias and the fleshy strap-like leaves may reach 2 ft (60 cm) in length, but the incredible flower production more than compensates. A single plant in a 5 in. (13 cm) pot may well carry 150 or more flowers at one time during the summer months. In winter, streptocarpus should be kept in a cool room, where the temperature does not fall below 45°F (7°C), and watered occasionally, only when the leaves droop and begin to become limp. In the absence of a greenhouse, repotting is best carried out at the end of March. Remove as much as possible of the old compost, dividing the plant if necessary (see p. 17), and pot into clean pots using a mixture of equal volumes of moss peat and John Innes no. 2 potting compost. This suggested potting material is the one I use, but others are suitable, bearing in mind that free drainage is an essential and that the compost must have an open texture: if it packs down after a while and the surface becomes impervious to air, the fibrous root system of the plant will probably rot and the plant will just fall out of the compost.

Achimenes, sometimes offered in garden centres as house-plants, make a very colourful show during the summer months. They should be grown in light but not sunny positions and fed regularly with high potash fertilizer. Particular care should be taken that they are not left bone dry for any length of time, especially during the early part of their growth. In the autumn, of course, flowering will stop and the foliage begins to die down. At this time they are rather messy and are best removed to a green-house, where the underground rhizomes are allowed to develop (see p. 18). However, if no greenhouse is available, the drying-off can be carried out in a cool spare room and the pots of rhizomes stored frost-free over the winter. The same treatment applies to the florist's gloxinia. Here, though, we are dealing with a much larger plant, up to 2 ft (60 cm) across, with a mass of huge trumpet flowers produced from the centre for a couple of months. After flowering, the plant again needs to be slowly dried off, leaving a quite large tuber, up to 4 in. (10 cm) in diameter, to be stored until the following spring.

All the gesneriads require good light to flower well and lack of light is often a cause of disappointment with their performance. They are, however, very amenable to culture under artificial lights indoors. The use of fluorescent lighting to give 12 to 14 hours of illumination each day can result in a much longer flowering period for most gesneriads, particularly saintpaulias, and in conjunction with terrarium-type containers, it enables such beautiful plants as the episcias to be grown. The light tubes may be of the warm white type, fixed 10 in. (25 cm) or so above the plants, but please ensure that they are fitted by a qualified electrician. With light gardens and terrariums, it is possible to grow exotic plants in ideal conditions and they can transform an otherwise dark corner of a room into a showpiece. It is well worth reading one of the books on the subject (see p. 62).

IN A GREENHOUSE OR CONSERVATORY

In a greenhouse or conservatory shaded from the direct sun, a wide range of flowering gesneriads may be grown, depending on the temperature that can be maintained in the winter. If a temp-erature of 68°F (20°C) can be held, then all except perhaps the episcias will be possible. The many beautiful columneas will make great cascades of stems in a season or two if grown in

Opposite: 'Stavanger', one of the best known *Columnea* hybrids, is a spectacular hanging basket plant

'Paula', another of the series of *Streptocarpus* hybrids with girls' names

baskets suspended from the roof; nematanthus, with their curious clog-shaped flowers, form a permanent display, while streptocarpus will often flower throughout the year at the higher temperature. In such a conservatory, shading is necessary not only against direct sunlight, but also to keep the temperature down, since 85°F (30°C) is as high a temperature as most gesneriads will accept. Special care will be needed when watering in summer, for most if not all the plants will be in a very open peat-based compost, which will dry out quite rapidly in the higher temperatures. In the height of summer, some plants, especially those in hanging baskets, may require watering a couple of times a day. Achimenes in particular suffer a severe setback if they are allowed to dry out in the early stages of their growth, so watch any of these in the collection. It is a good idea to incorporate a small amount of live sphagnum moss in the compost (about a quarter of the volume of the compost) to improve its water-retaining capacity. The moss has the additional advantage that it contains iodine, which is a very effective fungicide.

In a cooler greenhouse, where 50°F (10°C) is maintained in winter, streptocarpus can form the main display in spring and autumn, with achimenes, sinningias and the florist's gloxinias in summer and saintpaulias added during the warmer months.

Propagation

Gesneriads can be propagated by a wide range of methods, as well as by seed. For the amateur, the best time of the year to increase stock by vegetative means is obviously during the warm months of summer when the plants are in active growth.

LEAF CUTTINGS

Saintpaulias are very easily propagated by leaf cuttings. Cut a mature leaf with 1½ in. (3 cm) or so of stem and pot it into a small pot of peat and sand mixture with half the length of stem submerged so that the leaf sits like a flag (see figure 1). The cutting is gently watered in and then treated like an adult plant, that is to say allowed to become almost dry before rewatering. I find that the best results are obtained by watering with a half-strength liquid fertilizer solution rather than plain water. By feeding like this, there seems to be less tendency for the leaf to wilt and the callus (the tissue from which the new roots develop) at the base of the stalk is produced more quickly.

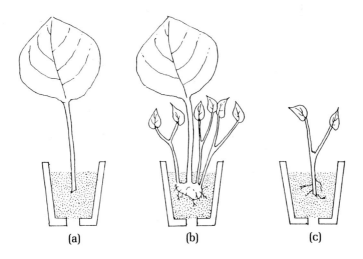

(a)   (b)   (c)

Figure 1: sequence of producing new plants from a leaf – (a) leaf potted into peat and sand mixture; (b) clump of plantlets forming from cut end of the stem; (c) plantlets removed and potted singly

In summer, when a temperature of 70°F (21°C) may be expected, leaves will usually root in two to three weeks and small plantlets appear after a total of six weeks. When the clump of plantlets is about 1 in. (2.5 cm) high, the leaf should be tipped out of its pot, the compost shaken off and the plantlets carefully teased apart. They are then potted into separate small pots or spaced 1 in. (2.5 cm) apart in a seed tray in a peat and sand mixture, to be grown on for a few weeks before potting into 3½ in. (9 cm) pots containing moss peat and John Innes no. 2 compost. I personally prefer to put the plantlets individually into 2 in. (5 cm) square pots, since this affords the least disturbance when potting on and allows for variations in growth between different plantlets.

Other gesneriads may be propagated using leaves complete with the petiole or leaf stalk. With some of the tuberous-rooted types, like the florist's gloxinia and the Sinningia species, it will be found that a small tuber is formed at the bottom of the leaf stalk. This tiny tuber needs to be given a dryish dormant period before it is started into growth in spring, in the same way as a full-sized tuber (see p. 58). The leaf cutting may also be taken without any stem, cutting across the base of the leaf, when the parent leaf will produce plantlets from the ends of the cut veins below the soil (see figure 2a). These should be grown on to increase in size and often flower before entering a dormant stage, having produced a small tuber during the growth period.

(a) (b)

Figure 2: types of leaf cuttings – (a) leaf cut across the base (Streptocarpus, Sinningia); (b) leaf cut in half longitudinally (Streptocarpus)

Leaf cuttings are also used to propagate named forms of Streptocarpus. One method is to cut across the leaves to form sections of leaf 2 in. (5 cm) deep, which are planted to half their depth in a peat and sand mixture, with the leaf edge from nearest the parent plant below the compost (see figure 2b). Alternatively, a leaf is trimmed first top and bottom and the main rib is then cut out to give two long half-leaves, which are potted edgewise into a seed tray of peat and sand. In either case, the leaves should not be enclosed in polythene but left open and treated as a normal plant, allowing them to almost dry out between watering with half-strength liquid fertilizer solution. If the leaves are planted some time between the end of April and the end of June, no additional heat will be required whether they are in a greenhouse or on the kitchen windowsill. Plantlets often appear in six to eight weeks, to be divided and potted singly into small pots using just sphagnum moss peat as the potting medium. If fed with a high potash feed at every other watering and grown in a light but not sunny position, the majority of these young plants will flower before the end of summer.

STEM CUTTINGS

The most convenient way to make new plants of the trailing species, like *Aeschynanthus*, *Columnea* and *Nematanthus*, is by stem cuttings. Without a heated propagator, this is best done in June, July and August, when the cuttings will root easily in pots of moss peat or a peat and sand mixture without any additional heat. In a heated propagator, of course, the cuttings will root at almost any time of year if a bottom heat of 77°F (25°C) can be maintained. Take a piece of stem 3–6 in. (7.5–15 cm) long, remove the lower two or three leaves and plant five cuttings to a 3½ in. (9 cm) pot, where they will root in three or four weeks. Once they are growing away, they can be stopped by pinching off at a length of about 6 in. (15 cm), which will induce new breaks from most of the leaf axils and give the basis of a strong bushy plant. This should be potted on into an 8 in. (20 cm) basket or a 5½ in. (14 cm) half-pot, using a compost made up of equal volumes of moss peat and John Innes no. 2, with perhaps the addition of some leafmould.

DIVISION

Many of the gesneriads, particularly *Streptocarpus* and *Saintpaulia*, will form multi-headed plants if left to themselves. When this happens, the plant not only looks unsightly, but there is a greatly increased chance of mould forming in the congested centre, leading to the collapse of the entire plant. It is necessary, therefore, and quite easy to divide such a plant. When the plant is tipped out of its pot, there will be obvious division points where the clump may be cut through – in fact, with streptocarpus, the plant may almost fall to pieces by itself. Otherwise, cut the plant through using a sharp knife, through the root ball as well if necessary. These divisions should then be cleaned of any broken or loose pieces and potted individually into pots of moss peat. Water them carefully until they begin to show obvious signs of growth, at which time they can be potted on into suitable-sized pots of moss peat and John Innes no. 2 and grown on to flower. Any spare leaves that may become separated during the division process can be used for leaf cuttings if further young plants are required. The whole operation is best performed in spring, at the beginning of the growing season.

My personal opinion is that all gesneriads are best propagated and new plants grown at least every other year, if not annually. Young plants seem to flower much more freely than plants that have become rather woody at the base, possibly because this restricts the free flow of sap to the newer growths.

STOLON ROSETTES

Some gesneriads, including the trailing saintpaulias and the episcias, form new rosettes at the ends of wiry stems or stolons. These give us a foolproof method of propagation. If each rosette is simply potted into a small pot of moss peat, while still attached to the parent plant by its stolon, and kept watered, the rosette will form its own roots in a matter of three or four weeks, when the stolon may be severed and the new plant grown on without any disturbance. Trailing African violets can be rooted freely during the summer months, while episcias may be rooted at almost any time of the year, bearing in mind the high temperature requirements of the latter.

RHIZOME DIVISION

Those gesneriads which form scaly rhizomes under the soil usually make several new rhizomes from a single original, which can be simply potted up as separate plants. If a rhizome of, say, an achimenes is planted and the complete cycle of growth, flowering and ripening to final dryness is followed (see p. 52), it will be found that the original rhizome has disappeared and that new rhizomes have developed on thin runners from the stem below the soil level. Occasionally, rhizomes may also be produced from leaf axils above the soil. These rhizomes are made up of over-

Opposite: *Episcia cupreata* is easily propagated from stolon rosettes

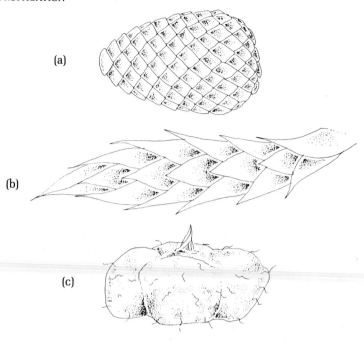

(a)

(b)

(c)

Figure 3: types of root systems – (a) catkin-like rhizome (*Achimenes, Smithiantha*); (b) long scaly rhizome (*Koehleria*); (c) tuber (*Sinningia*)

lapping scales and, in the case of *Achimenes*, are like small catkins in appearance. *Smithiantha* are somewhat similar but generally larger and often a little more open, while *Koehleria* and *Gloxinia* form long winding rhizomes with the scales spaced at intervals along their length. The increase in the number of rhizomes with *Achimenes* and *Smithiantha* means that more plants can be added to the collection each season. In the case of *Koehleria* and *Gloxinia*, the long rhizomes may be broken into pieces about 2 in. (5 cm) long and potted up individually when plants are repotted to start into growth in the spring. As a bonus, every scale on the rhizome of all gesneriads in this group will, if potted, start into growth and make a small plant to go through its growing cycle and form a new rhizome, even if the plant itself is not strong enough to flower in its first season; in this way, new plants may be obtained in a season or two. These rhizomatous gesneriads may also be increased during the growing season by stem cuttings (see p. 17).

Tuberous "gloxinias" may be propagated by tuber division or leaf cuttings

TUBER DIVISION

Tuberous gesneriads may be increased by cutting tubers across if they produce several shoots. A careful watch is needed for when the new growths are starting to appear at the top of the tuber in spring. When these are about 2 in. (5 cm) high, the tuber may be cut cleanly across with a sharp knife to leave one shoot to each piece of tuber. The cut surfaces should then be dusted with sulphur dust to minimize the risk of fungal growth and left for a day before potting into a peat and sand mixture for the tuber to form roots. An alternative to this rather drastic procedure is again to wait for the tuber to produce new shoots and, when these are about 3 in. (7.5 cm) high with a few leaves formed, to remove them carefully with a sideways pressure. They are easily detached like this and can be potted individually into small pots of moss peat, where they will root in a couple of weeks to be potted on as needed. An old tuber will often produce new growths in succession over a period of several weeks. The miniature *Sinningia* are easily propagated by this method.

SEED

All members of this family are readily grown from seed and most will flower within a year of sowing. Since the seed is very fine, some care should be taken in preparing the container. Fill a pan or small seed tray to about two thirds of its depth with a mixture of moss peat and sand, damp this down and slightly firm it. On top of this sprinkle a thin layer of fine sphagnum moss, prepared by rubbing it between the hands when bone dry and then sieving it through a tea strainer. The layer of moss gives an excellent surface for sowing which allows some air circulation around the seeds and, because of the iodine in the moss, it also acts as a deterrent to fungal growths.

The seed is sown as evenly as possible over the surface of the moss, the tray covered with a sheet of glass or polythene and the whole put into a propagator at 77°F (25°C). Germination takes place in seven to fourteen days in most cases. As the seedlings become visible, the cover on the tray should be gradually removed, but the tray kept in the propagator. The seedlings are very tiny at first and should be very carefully watered with a fine spray as used for misting. A half-strength liquid fertilizer solution can be incorporated in the water after the first week. Once the seedlings have made two tiny leaves, growth seems to speed up and, when they are $\frac{1}{2}$ in. (1.2 cm) across, they are robust enough to be transplanted individually into 2 in. (5 cm) pots of peat and sand mixture. The pots may be kept in the propagator for a week or so to settle down and the seedlings should then be gradually hardened off in a shady position in the house or greenhouse and finally potted on when large enough to their flowering size pots, which will be determined by the size and type of the plant, in a compost of moss peat and John Innes no. 2.

Opposite: *Smithiantha* hybrids increase naturally by forming new rhizomes

Pests and diseases

PESTS

The usual range of pests can attack gesneriads, but with modern insecticides they are not much of a problem, particularly if a systemic insecticide is used, which is taken up into the sap of the plant to act from within and destroy the insect pests as they feed. I find that watering once a month with a systemic insecticide will keep the plants free from almost every pest.

Mealybug is indicated by small patches like white cotton-wool, usually in the leaf axils or on the undersides of the leaves. The insect itself is quite mobile and can move freely from plant to plant, multiplying rapidly and sometimes hiding in odd crevices in woodwork or elsewhere. If these insects are found, it is advisable to spray the area around the plants with insecticide, as well as treating the plants themselves, and to do so without delay. Some plants seem to be particularly attractive hosts to mealybug; *Hoya* and *Passiflora* are apparently strong favourites and often show signs of the insect before any other plant.

Root mealybug is only detectable when a plant is tipped out of its pot and then shows as a white woolly covering on some of the roots, with wool-covered insects often to be seen in the surrounding soil. This and the ordinary mealybug have a waxy protective coating, which makes them difficult to eradicate with normal insecticides, but both are vulnerable to systemic insecticides.

Aphids or greenfly are frequently found on new growths and especially on flower stems and buds. If untreated, *Streptocarpus* seem to attract large numbers on the flowers during early summer. Control is very effective with systemic insecticides.

Insecticides, however, are not effective against vine weevil. This is one of the most versatile pests, feeding upon almost any plant. The adult beetle is a hard-shelled insect which feeds at night, generally on the leaves of plants. Although slow-moving, it travels quite long distances, wandering from greenhouse to garden and back, and is often found indoors. Since the adult beetle can lay up to a thousand eggs in its lifetime, the larvae may occur anywhere in the garden or in pots, where they create havoc, eating first the roots and then other parts of the plant, burrowing into stems and tubers alike.

The first sign of the presence of larvae in a pot is when the plant stops growing for no apparent reason, which is followed by drooping foliage and finally collapse and complete disintegration. At this stage, if an attacked plant is taken hold of by the top, it will come away from the pot and all of it below soil level will have been eaten away. If, however, at the early signs of the plant stopping growth it is tipped out of the pot and the soil carefully removed, the pest can be seen as one or more small grub-like larvae, which are white with brown heads. These should be disposed of and the plant repotted using fresh compost, and in the majority of cases the plant will form new roots and recover. Vine weevil may be deterred to some extent by incorporating gamma-BHC or HCH dust in the compost when potting, but complete prevention is not possible.

Tarsonemid mite is a minute pest, invisible to the naked eye, which affects gesneriads as well as other plants. It is evidenced by the shrivelling of new growth and often of the new buds, which become dust-dry and brown before reaching maturity. None of the insecticides available to amateur gardeners will control this pest and infested plants should be burnt. Ensure that newly acquired plants are healthy, if necessary keeping them in quarantine for a few weeks.

DISEASES

Attacks by fungal growths, botrytis in particular, are usually due to bad management, when plants have been kept under conditions of high humidity with inadequate air circulation, particularly if the temperature has been low. Good housekeeping is the cure. Do not overwater plants or keep them in close conditions; do not allow plants like African violets to become congested in their pots; and do not let old leaves and blossoms rot and decay on or around the plants.

Saintpaulia

There are about twenty species of *Saintpaulia*, mainly from Tanzania in central Africa, which are of two types. The first forms virtually stemless rosettes of fleshy stemmed, thick, hairy leaves, which make congested clumps if left to themselves, and bear upright flower stems from the leaf axils carrying two to ten mauve or white flowers with prominent yellow anthers. These are the basic species that have been developed into our modern range of African violets. The second type has thin, wiry, trailing stems with alternate leaves along their length and flowers also produced on stems from the leaf axils. The flowers have a short tube and two upright upper petals and three larger, lower, lobed petals which gave a fairly flat face to the flower.

The species themselves are not often seen but, with the vast amount of work that has been carried out on this genus, there is now an enormous range of plants to choose from, including rosettes, miniatures and trailing kinds. Flowers may be red, pink, white, blue, purple or bicolored, single or double, many with ruffled edges to the petals. The foliage also shows many variations in colour. White flowers are generally associated with light green leaves with a silvery white underside, while dark-coloured flowers go with dark green leaves having a red underside. Leaf shapes vary too, flat smooth-edged leaves and crinkle-edged leaves being the more simple variants. Added to this are the different sorts of variegated leaf. 'Tommie Lou' is one of the best of a group with cream-edged green leaves, and there are others with yellow or even pink edges. The Mosaic section has, as the name suggests, cream or light green streaks in the central area of the leaves. A third group produces cream or pink leaves and stems from the centre of the rosette, which gradually change to green as they mature. The first two types of variegation seem to be quite stable under normal growing conditions, but the third appears to produce the light-coloured new leaves only when the temperature is below 68°F (20°C).

After World War II, the potential of the African violet was realized as a compact flowering houseplant and commercial growers started to produce them in huge quantities, with Thomas Rochford leading the field in England. The Rhapsodie series of very free-flowering plants in a wide range of colours began to dominate the market, followed by the Ballet series, with an

Tony Clements' *Saintpaulia* exhibit won a Gold Medal at the Chelsea Show in 1988

improved ability to hold the flowers, and recently the Rococo plants with newer forms of flower. Even more developments can be expected in the future, with work being carried out by Joan Hill, a well known amateur grower, and by the commercial nursery of Tony Clements in Britain, as well as by many others abroad, notably in Europe and North America.

The rosette-type saintpaulias should be grown as a single rosette, using a peat-based compost with very free drainage. A suitable mixture is two parts of moss peat, one part of John Innes no. 2 and one part of perlite or coarse grit by volume. Water only when the compost is fairly dry and ideally grow them where a winter minimum temperature of 68°F (20°C) can be maintained. A few degrees lower will not worry the plants unduly, provided they are kept on the dry side, but the higher temperature will en-

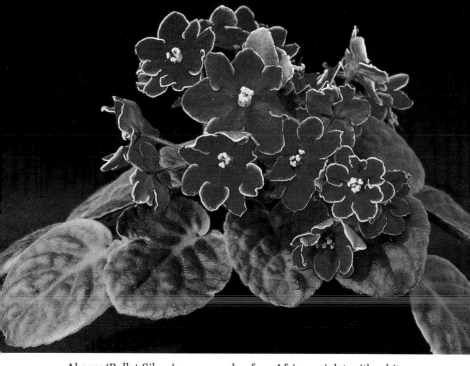

Above: 'Ballet Silver', an example of an African violet with white-rimmed flowers
Below: the new miniature African violets have aroused much interest

courage free production of flowers. Feed with a high potash (tomato-type) fertilizer at every other watering during the flowering season, and once every two months flush the pot through with several changes of water to prevent the build up of salts in the compost, which can lead to souring of the soil and eventual loss of roots and subsequent death of the plant. This occasional wash-through of the pot is advisable for all plants grown in pots.

Good light is required for maximum flowering and flowers are borne at any time of the year for several months at a time. A day length of 12 to 14 hours is the optimum, so supplementary lighting is obviously an advantage during the winter months. When flowers cease to appear, the plant should be tipped out of its pot, all the old soil shaken off, the plant divided if necessary and old damaged leaves removed by a sideways pressure so that the leaf stalk and leaf come away cleanly from the stem. The plant is then repotted, setting the main stem slightly lower in the compost so that there is no bare stem above the compost, into a 4 in. (10 cm) pot and in a mixture of moss peat and John Innes no. 2 compost. With the plant free of flowers, use a high nitrogen fertilizer for the first four to six weeks, to develop good foliage, and then return to a high potash feed for flower initiation and production. Any divisions may be treated in the same way and any small side-shoots removed at the time of repotting should be potted in a similar manner, into a pot size corresponding to the size of the off-shoot. Some of the undamaged leaves taken off at repotting can be used for propagation and, if potted as leaf cuttings at a temperature of 70–80°F (21–26°C), they will make flowering plants in $3\frac{1}{2}$ in. (9 cm) pots after about six months (see p. 15).

The trailing saintpaulias are excellent hanging basket plants, graceful in habit, with new rosettes produced on wiry stolons soon giving a well-clothed appearance to the basket (see p. 31). Propagation is easily carried out by rooting rosettes into 2 in. (5 cm) pots of moss peat while their stolons are still attached to the parent plant, the stolon being severed about three weeks later when the rosette will have formed its own roots (see p. 18).

The miniatures are a more recent development, growing only 2 in. (5 cm) across, with a rather more open manner of growth than the standard rosette-type. As yet there is not the colour range of the larger kinds, but no doubt this will be seen in the future. Treat them in the same way as normal African violets.

All the saintpaulias are excellent flowering plants for the house, warm greenhouse or conservatory in light but not sunny positions. There is now an incredible range available, all very floriferous, and the selection is a matter of personal preference for flower colour and habit.

Saintpaulia shumensis has been used in the Endurance hybrids

Saintpaulia confusa.   A small species from moist regions in the East Usambara mountains in Tanzania. It has light green, rather thin leaves, slightly toothed on the margins, green beneath, with the hairs on the leaf surfaces flattened down and somewhat silky, not erect. The small, pale violet-blue flowers have a darker centre.

S. ionantha.   Found in warm, very humid areas near Tanga in Tanzania. With *S. confusa*, it is the parent of most of our modern hybrids. The leaves are dark green with a bronze cast, hairy, reddish on the undersides. Flowers are violet, 1 in. (2.5 cm) across.

S. shumensis.   This comes from dry forest areas in the West Usambara mountains in Tanzania, at fairly high elevations, so may withstand cooler conditions than most other species. It is a small plant with quite thick, light green leaves lightly covered with long white hairs. Small mauve or blue flowers with a violet eye.

S. 'Blue Boy'.   One of the first hybrids, between *S. ionantha* and *S. confusa*, developed about 1930 in America. It is a very floriferous plant with single violet-blue flowers from a rosette of fresh green leaves.

S. 'Snow White'.   The first white hybrid, originating as a sport from 'Blue Boy' in 1941. A rather flat rosette of small green leaves with large quantities of single white flowers.

Above: 'Fancy Pants', a delightful African violet with bicolored ruffle-edged flowers
Below: trailing African violets, with their neat manner of growth, are ideal for hanging baskets

Modern hybrids. Among these, there are a few which, in my opinion, ought to be in every collection – 'Fancy Pants', with frilled-edged magenta and white flowers (see p. 31); 'Rococo Pink', for a profusion of double pink flowers (see cover); 'Garden News', having white blooms flushed delicately with mauve; and 'Ballet Silver', which has a very large, blue, star-shaped flower edged with white (see p. 28). It really is difficult, though, to recommend which ones to grow. The best plan is to visit a specialist nursery and select plants from the enormous variety usually in stock (see p. 62).

Finally, it will not come amiss to repeat the basic rules of successful culture of African violets. First, keep them warm: in a temperature where human beings are warm and comfortable, the plants will also be happy. Second, grow them in a position where they will get strong light but not direct sunlight and, for maximum flower production, extend the light period to 12 to 14 hours if possible, with supplementary fluorescent lighting in the short winter days. Third, make sure they are kept out of cold draughts and are not placed near a fire or radiator where they might receive radiant heat. Fourth, grow them in a free-draining compost and do not keep the pot soaking wet all the time, but allow the compost to dry out between watering. Fifth, feed with a high potash fertilizer. Finally, grow the plants as single rosettes and do not let dead leaves or flowers remain around the plant; keep them clean and divide when growth has become congested.

'Garden News', a striking white African violet

Streptocarpus

This African genus has been grown in England since the mid-1800s and contains both annuals and perennials. It may be divided into plants that produce large, fleshy, almost primula-like leaves – the "true" Streptocarpus, sometimes called Cape primrose – and a smaller number of plants of branched shrubby growth, known as Streptocarpella. A characteristic of streptocarpus is that the leaves grow in a continuous manner from the base, so that if growth is halted for any reason and there is a discontinuity in the leaf, this defect will gradually grow away from the bottom of the leaf. The leaves can reach a length of 3 ft (90 cm) in some cases and the flowers are produced on erect stems in succession, arising from a point where a thick stem-like section joins the leaf itself to the fibrous root system. Most of the species which produce only one large leaf are annuals and must therefore be propagated from seed, which is quite freely produced in long, twisted seed capsules. One or two of the single-leaved species are exceptional in that they sometimes make an odd leaf on the base of the parent, which develops roots while still on the old leaf, and these may be detached and potted to make a new plant. The species that are most widely cultivated, however, form a number of leaves from a strong fibrous root system, to make a dense clump, and produce spikes of flowers in succession over a long period from each leaf. These plants are perennial and have been hybridized to give a very wide range of colours.

In the 1930s, a number of species were hybridized at the John Innes Institute, resulting in the famous Streptocarpus 'Constant Nymph', which shows the influence of one of its parents, S. johannis, in its multi-flowered habit and in the flat pansy-type flower with a thin tube. In 1966, X-ray irradiation of 'Constant Nymph' gave rise to darker forms with marbled flowers, while a white-flowered form, 'Maassen's White', made its appearance in the Netherlands. In 1969, A.G. Brown, at the John Innes Institute, carried out more hybridization work and obtained a range of plants with pink, violet and magenta flowers, which were given girls' names such as 'Paula' and 'Tina' (see p. 14). These all have the "pansy" flower of 'Constant Nymph', combined with the ability to produce hundreds of flowers in a season extending from April to November. In West Germany, an alternative line of approach to hybridization led to the Wiesmoor series in 1952.

These have several-flowered spikes bearing large tubular flowers with broad open lobes in a range of colours from white to pink, red and violet, often with coloured markings on the lower lobes.

The future will probably see a great deal of development in *Streptocarpus*, particularly to produce smaller-growing types. Present plants need a considerable amount of space and a plant in a 5 in. (13 cm) pot can easily attain a spread of 2 ft (60 cm). Even so, their ease of culture and the enormous quantity of flowers produced mean that streptocarpus are becoming more and more widely grown as ornamental pot plants.

In the home, conservatory or greenhouse, streptocarpus are best grown in an open peat-based compost in a light but not sunny position and allowed to dry out almost completely between watering. Since the plants make a mass of fibrous roots, the best way to ensure the soil ball is wetted right through is to immerse the pot in a bowl of water and leave it to stand there for 15 minutes or so before draining. Use a high potash fertilizer at every other watering while the plants are in active growth and flush the pot through with clear water every couple of months to minimize any build up of salts in the compost. Comparatively cool conditions suit these plants, with 50–70°F (10–21°C) an ideal range. They will withstand 40°F (7°C) in winter if kept fairly dry, although a warm winter temperature of 60°F (15°C) will often result in a number of flowers appearing all through the winter.

Propagation may be by seed sown in February in a propagator at 70°F (21°C) (see p. 22), to produce plants which will bear a few flowers the same autumn. For named varieties, though, old plants may be divided in spring and early summer, or leaf cuttings may be taken at any time of the year when the temperature is above 60°F(15°C) (see pp. 17 and 15). From leaf cuttings, there is always the possibility of a vegetative sport appearing, as there is with saintpaulias.

Of the plants placed under *Streptocarpella*, *S. saxorum* is the most widely grown (see p. 37). It forms a well-branched shrub with succulent stems up to 18 in. (45 cm) tall and 1 in. (2.5 cm) thick, hairy, grey-green leaves. From the leaf axils, in spring and early summer, flowers are produced singly on 3 in. (7.5 cm) wiry stems, each flower 1 in. (2.5 cm) across, bright violet with a white throat. The plant needs a high light intensity but not direct sun and, as is obvious from its very succulent appearance, does not like to be kept too damp. It is best propagated by stem cuttings in moss peat during the summer (see p. 17).

Opposite: the *Streptocarpus* exhibit by Dibley's Efenechtyd Nurseries at the Chelsea Show, 1989, which received a Gold Medal

Opposite above: 'Constant Nymph' paved the way for later
Streptocarpus hybrids; below: *Streptocarpus* 'Maassen's White' is still
one of the best white-flowered hybrids
Above: *Streptocarpella saxorum*, an interesting shrubby species with
fleshy stems and leaves; below: *Streptocarpus candidus* has honey-
scented flowers

Above: the prolific flowering habit of *Streptocarpus johannis* has been inherited by many of the hybrids
Below: like other *Streptocarpus* hybrids, 'Tina' flowers over a very long period

Streptocarpus candidus. Forms a clump, with leaves 18 by 6 in. (45 × 15 cm). Many-flowered spikes of 1 in. (2.5 cm) flowers, white with yellow stripes and purple spots in the throat and two purple lines at the base of the lip (see p. 37).

S. johannis. Clump-forming, with many leaves up to 18 by 4 in. (45 × 10 cm). Erect stems bearing ¾ in. (1.8 cm) pale blue-mauve flowers with a thin tube, whitish in the centre, are freely produced, with anything up to 30 flowers on a stem.

S. rexii. The first species to be discovered, in 1828, this has been used extensively in the production of hybrids. It forms a clump of 12 by 3 in. (30 × 7.5 cm) leaves and has 8 in. (20 cm) flower spikes, with two to six 1½ in. (4 cm) flowers, which are white suffused with mauve and with seven violet stripes from the throat onto the lower lip.

S. wendlandii. This species produces just one leaf, 2 ft by 10 in. (60 × 25 cm), with a thick stalk at the base. The upright flower stems carry 2 in. (5 cm) violet flowers with two dark purple blotches and a white stripe in the throat (see p. 36).

S. 'Constant Nymph'. Makes a clump of green strap-shaped leaves up to 18 by 3 in. (45 × 7.5 cm), corrugated in texture with depressed veins. Two to eight 2 in. (5 cm) flowers are borne to a stem, deep violet blue with darker veining on the lower lobes and yellow-white in the throat (see p. 36).

S. 'Helen'. A fairly compact clump of 12 in. (30 cm) leaves. The 6 in. (15 cm) flower stems carry ten to fifteen violet-blue flowers with darker veining on the lower lobes and a white throat.

S. 'Karen'. Leaves up to 16 in. (40 cm) long. Each stem carries six to ten flowers, 2 in. (5 cm) across, pansy-type, magenta pink with darker shading and dark veins on the lower lobes extending into the throat (see p. 6).

S. 'Maassen's White'. Makes a clump of leaves up to 2 ft (60 cm) across. The pansy-like flowers are pure white with a tinge of pale yellow in the throat, four to twelve in each spray (see p. 36).

S. 'Tina'. Six to sixteen pink flowers on 6 in. (15 cm) stems, with paler pink upper petals. The lower petals have darker veining.

Streptocarpella saxorum. See p. 35.

Fibrous-rooted gesneriads

AESCHYNANTHUS

These tropical vines, usually found as epiphytes on trees in southeast Asia, are ideal for growing in hanging baskets in a very open compost. A mixture of equal parts of sphagnum moss peat and coarse sand or perlite is best, possibly with some chopped sphagnum moss incorporated. The plants produce strong stems, often several feet long in some species, and bear clusters of brilliant red, orange, yellow or brown flowers, some species in the leaf axils, others at the end of the stems.

Fairly high temperatures and humidity are required for the best results and a greenhouse or conservatory with a winter minimum of 68°F (20°C) or higher is really necessary. However, a number of species and some hybrids are imported and sold as houseplants, and seem to be very good in that capacity until they outgrow their space. They are easily renewed by young plants. Since in nature the stems often root along their length, it is no problem to root cuttings at a temperature of 75°F (24°C) (see p. 17); if cuttings 6 in. (15 cm) or so long are rooted in spring, they will probably flower at the tips during the summer. Five or six such cuttings in a pot is the usual form in which plants are available from the florist or nursery.

Flowering is mainly during the summer months. After flowering, the stems branch quite freely and plants should be potted on into a basket, when the stems may be cut back as required to keep them within bounds. Hang the basket in strong light but shaded from direct sun through glass. Water freely while growing and use a high potash fertilizer at every other watering.

Aeschynanthus lobbianus. Strong arching stems with small, dark green, opposite, thick, fleshy leaves and clusters of 2 in. (5 cm) brilliant crimson flowers emerging from purple-brown tubular calyces, with pale yellow patterning in the throat. The stems will grow up to 3 ft (90 cm) in length, so plenty of room is needed if the plant is not stopped fairly often.
A. longicaulis (A. marmoratus). More flexible stems, drooping over the sides of a pot or basket quite freely, with shiny, pointed,

Opposite: Aeschynanthus species are good plants for a hanging basket

41

light green leaves marbled with brown on the upper surface and red on the underneath. The 1 in. (2.5 cm) flowers are orange and green.

A. nanus. A trailer with small, waxy, light green leaves and showy flowers of vermilion-red with a yellow throat.

Figure 4: *Aeschynanthus nanus*

A. pulcher. This species from Java is very similar to *A. lobbianus*, but somewhat stronger in general habit, with larger flowers which have the calyces tipped with green. Very easily rooted from cuttings.

CHIRITA

Most of the species in this genus are shrubby and are not often seen. However, one that is different and very striking in appearance is *Chirita sinensis* (see also p. 25). It is usually raised from seed sown at 68°F (20°C) and grown on in a peat-based compost to form a flat rosette of ten to twelve leaves, borne in opposite pairs on a very short stem. The leaves are 6 by 3 in. (15 × 7.5 cm), oval, very thick and succulent, dark green with a pattern of broad silver along the veins giving a marbled effect. Rather small lilac

Opposite: *Chirita sinensis*, an unusual rosette-forming gesneriad from southern China

Above: *Columnea hirta*, a Costa Rican species with stiffly trailing stems
Below: the flowers of *Columnea schiedeana* open in spring and summer

flowers are produced on 2 in. (5 cm) stems from the leaf axils in late summer. Bright light is needed to maintain good leaf colouration. Leaf cuttings may be used to propagate the plant (see p. 15). Occasionally, a small plant will develop from one of the lower leaf axils of a mature specimen, which may be taken off and will root quite easily in a small pot of moss peat.

COLUMNEA

This is a genus of well over 100 species from the American tropical region, which are epiphytic in nature, mostly trailing in habit. They have proved adaptable to culture as houseplants and a number of species are available commercially, as well as some fine hybrids. The flowers are generally red to yellow, tubular, opening out with the upper lobes extended and broadened to form a hood over the lower lobes. The fruits are smooth round berries, usually white, filled with small smooth seeds, which germinate freely if sown at a temperature of 77°F (25°C) (see p. 22).

The plants are grown in a compost made up of equal volumes of moss peat and perlite with the addition of half a part of chopped sphagnum moss. Water freely during the summer and feed with a high potash fertilizer at every other watering while in active growth, with the temperature maintained at 60–86°F (15–30°C) and some shading from the direct sunlight. During the winter only a little water will be needed and the plants make minimal growth then. Propagation is carried out by means of stem cuttings of six or eight joints rooted in pots of moss peat during the summer, when ambient temperatures are fairly high and the plants are growing freely (see p. 17).

Columnea gloriosa.   A trailing species from Costa Rica which is an excellent basket plant. The trailing stems branch freely, growing to several feet in length, with 1 in. (2.5 cm) oval, hairy, light green leaves. The red and yellow flowers have the upper lobe extended to form a red helmet over the lower lobes, and flowers may be produced at odd times throughout the year. The subspecies *atropurpurea* has purple hairy leaves.

C. hirta.   A shrubby plant of red-hairy stems and small, green, hairy leaves. The 2 in. (5 cm) orange-red flowers appear in the leaf axils in spring.

C. linearis.   An upright shrub from Costa Rica, up to 2 ft (60 cm) high, branching freely with long, narrow, 3½ in. (9 cm) leaves. The pink flowers are quite hairy and may be produced at any time.

C. microphylla.   Another trailing Costa Rican plant with small, oval, pointed, hairy, green leaves on pendent stems up to 6 ft (1.8 m) long. The orange-red hooded flowers have a bright yellow throat up to 3 in. (7.5 cm) long and are carried in large numbers in spring.

C. schiedeana. A rather lax-stemmed branching shrub from Mexico, with stems up to 3 ft (90 cm) long carrying somewhat hairy, 4 in. (10 cm), oval leaves. Orange-red flowers are 2 in. (5 cm) long, with a large helmet and a very narrow lower lobe (see p. 44).

C. 'Banksii'. An older hybrid with smooth green, almost succulent, 1 in. (2.5 cm), oval leaves on 3 ft (90 cm) stems. Orange-red flowers have a yellow throat. A variegated silver-leaved form is quite often seen (see p. 63).

Modern hybrids. There are now a number of hybrids on the market, produced no doubt to grow under the same sort of conditions as the African violet. Some of the better known are C. 'Stavanger', a basket plant with 4 in. (10 cm) red flowers with a yellow throat (see p. 12); C. 'Yellow Dragon', trailing, with the green leaves tinged red and the yellow flowers shaded red on the edge; and C. 'Alpha', a compound much-branched plant, with 2 in. (5 cm) pale yellow flowers produced all year round.

EPISCIA AND ALSOBIA

Episcia is a small genus of beautiful-leaved trailing or creeping plants from Central America. They need conditions of high temperature and high humidity, with light shade, and free drainage to the roots as afforded by a compost containing about half its volume of live sphagnum moss. Terrarium culture with a minimum temperature of 68°F (20°C) is therefore the most suitable. The broad oval leaves are variously coloured with brown, green and silver, downy haired, with a metallic sheen to the upper surface. New plants are produced at the ends of numerous stolons, which grow from the leaf axils. These new plants root readily and may be set into 3 in. (7.5 cm) pots of peat to root, before being severed from the parent plant (see p. 18). Most species and hybrids have brilliant red tubular flowers for almost all the year. Mature leaves can be used as leaf cuttings (see p. 15).

Episcia cupreata. Deep bronze-green leaves patterned with silver-green, with the surface quilted and covered with short dark hairs, red beneath. The flower tube is yellow with red spots, opening out to orange-red lobes. There are several named forms of this species with various leaf colourations (see also pp. 8 and 19).

E. reptans. Bronze-green leaves with green veins. The flower

Above: *Alsobia dianthiflora*, with its deeply fringed petals, is sometimes known as the lace flower
Below: forms of *Episcia cupreata* are notable for their varied leaf colours

tube is red on the outside, as are the large open lobes, with a white eye in the centre.

Modern hybrids.   In addition to the species, a large number of hybrids have been produced, mainly in America, which have a beautiful range of colour patterns on their leaves.

Alsobia dianthiflora *(E. dianthiflora)*.   Forms a rosette of many leaves, soft green, with scalloped edges, 2 in. (5 cm) across, producing quantities of offsets on long stolons. The plant makes a large mass of trailing rosettes, and 1 in. (2.5 cm) white flowers with fringed edges are produced all through the summer. The flowers have tiny purple spots in the throat. This species is easier to grow than the coloured-leaved varieties and makes a good basket plant in association with *Columnea* species and hybrids, doing well in the lower temperatures (see p. 47).

NEMATANTHUS

These are mostly trailing plants, rather like *Columnea* in habit, and many were known for a long time as *Hypocyrta*. They enjoy the same culture as columneas (see p. 45), but are distinguished mainly by their flowers, which hang from the stems on long stalks and often have the lobes incurved to leave only a small entrance to the flower. The glossy dark leaves make them quite attractive houseplants even when not in flower.

Nematanthus fritschii.   Arching 2 ft (60 cm) stems carry shiny green, 3 in. (7.5 cm), oval, pointed leaves with red undersides. The flower stems are hairy, very thin, 4 in. (10 cm) long, bearing bright pink flowers with a 2 in. (5 cm) long tube.

N. wettsteinii.   Previously known as *Hypocyrta glabra*, this is a basket plant with thin much-branched stems up to 3 ft (90 cm) long, having small, thick, oval, waxy, dark green leaves. The flowers are orange-red, shaded with yellow, 1 in. (2.5 cm) long, shiny, produced in quantity for almost all the year; their shape gives the plant its common name of clog plant.

N. 'Tropicana'.   One of a number of hybrids commercially available now. It was developed in the USA in 1969 and is a trailer with bronze-green, pointed, opposite leaves and deep yellow flowers marked with wavy orange-red lines. Very floriferous.

Opposite: *Nematanthus* 'Tropicana', one of the early hybrids, has itself been used in further breeding

Rhizomatous gesneriads

ACHIMENES

The first species of *Achimenes* was introduced into England in 1778 and was followed by many more from Central America in the 1800s. Sometimes known as hot water plants, they are essentially summer-flowering. They die down in the autumn and produce catkin-like scaly rhizomes beneath the soil to overwinter under dry conditions, thus providing several new plants (see p. 18). Individually, the plants are rather weak-stemmed and will droop over without any support; they should therefore be grown in a hanging basket to be seen to best advantage, with several plants to each container.

The flowers have a narrow tube, opening out to five flat rounded lobes, with a colour range of white, yellow, pink, red, blue and purple. They make marvellous flowering plants for the house, greenhouse or conservatory during the summer. When in growth, a temperature range of 60–77°F (15–25°C) is ideal, very high temperatures not being to their liking. A medium light intensity is needed, much as for African violets.

Achimenes hybrids (opposite and below) have vivid flowers appearing throughout the summer

Culture is easy. Pot up four or five rhizomes into a 3½ in. (9 cm) pot of a moist mixture of equal parts of moss peat and perlite or coarse sand, plus some lime chippings to increase the pH value of the compost. This may be done in April or May without the use of a heated propagator. There is then no need to water the pot until growth starts. Note that any small piece of a rhizome is worth potting, since it will sprout and form a plant. Once started into growth, keep the pots moist without letting them dry out for long and feed with a balanced fertilizer at every watering. Pot on as required and support the stems with split cane stakes if necessary. Blooming should commence about the end of May, to continue through until September.

In autumn, as the leaves begin to shrivel naturally, reduce the watering slowly and gradually allow the plants to dry out as the foliage becomes dead and the rhizomes form underground. When the plant has completely died down, the pot of rhizomes can be stored dry at a temperature of 50°F (10°C), or the rhizomes may be separated from the compost in the pot and stored at the same temperature in a box of peat.

Achimenes erecta. The first species introduced into England, from Mexico. The stems grow to 12 in. (30 cm) tall, with narrow, green, hairy leaves and quantities of ½ in. (1.2 cm) red flowers.

A. flava. Similar in habit to A. erecta, but the stems are weaker and tend to droop more easily. The flowers are deep yellow, spotted with red in the throat.

A. grandiflora. A Mexican species with erect 12 in. (30 cm) stems, bearing hairy green leaves shaded red on the underside. The 1½ in. (4 cm) flowers are dark red-purple with a white throat and red dots.

A. 'Purple King'. Very free-flowering over a long period, with deep purple-red flowers. One of the most widely available hybrids (see pp. 8, 50 and 51).

GLOXINIA

The true Gloxinia species are not the plants commonly known as gloxinias or florist's gloxinias, which are actually Sinningia speciosa or, these days, hybrids of that species (see p. 58). The real Gloxinia are typified by long-stemmed growths from scaly rhizomes, with flowers produced from the leaf axils in the summer months. All are from Central America and require similar treatment to Achimenes.

Gloxinia lindeniana. This species from Ecuador, earlier known

Gloxinia perennis is an attractive, easily grown houseplant

as *Koehleria lindeniana*, is easily raised from seed germinated at 68–77°F (20–25°C) and will flower in August from seed sown in February (see p. 22). The plant is upright, branched, up to 12 in. (30 cm) high, with 3 in. (7.5 cm) velvety leaves, dark red-brown with yellow veining on the main veins and flushed red beneath. The ¾ in. (2 cm) flowers are white with a mauve zone in the throat, produced from mid-July to the end of August. Water should be reduced after flowering and the plants kept almost dry at a minimum temperature of 50°F (10°C), then repotted and started into growth in March.

G. perennis. Erect-growing stems up to 2 ft (60 cm) high, with broad, oval, 5 by 4 in. (13 × 10 cm), green leaves having a wavy edge, lightly hairy and red beneath. The 1½ in. (2 cm) flowers are lavender with a dark spot in the throat and are produced from the leaf axils in June and July, after which the plants should be dried off slowly and stored dry until April of the next year, when the long rhizomes can be divided and repotted (see p. 18).

Koehleria eriantha (above and opposite), a shrubby species with striking flowers

G. sylvatica.   This species was collected in Peru in 1968. It has greyish stems up to 2 ft (60 cm) long, rather weak, which carry 4 in. (10 cm) grey-green leaves with a felt-like texture. The flowers are produced on thin 4 in. (10 cm) stems from the leaf axils of the new growths and are ¾ in. (2 cm) long, bright red, shaded orange with a yellow and red throat. At temperatures above 68°F (20°C), the plant does not seem to rest, but grows, flowers and produces new rhizomes constantly.

KOEHLERIA

The members of this genus are quite strong-growing plants, with hairy stems and colourful leaves, and are best grown in a temperature of 60–77°F (15–25°C), in as light a position as possible short of direct sunlight. The high light intensity gives sturdy erect growth and good leaf colour. They produce scaly rhizomes, not short and separate as in *Achimenes*, but long, branching and winding round the inside of the pot, often up to 18 in. (45 cm) long and ½ in. (1.2 cm) in diameter. These rhizomes should not be left bone dry for too long, even during the dormant period, when they will need watering about once a month if kept at 50°F (10°C). They may be broken up into pieces 2–3 in. (5–7.5 cm) long to increase stock when repotting in spring (see p. 18). The flowers are produced from the upper leaf axils in summer and they are very good plants for the conservatory or greenhouse.

Koehleria amabilis. Hairy stems up to 2 ft (60 cm) long, with whorls of 4 in. (10 cm), dark green, hairy leaves with purple veins. Rosy pink flowers with purple and brick-red spots on the lobes and throat in summer and autumn.

K. eriantha. An easily grown Colombian species, with deep green, hairy leaves, red beneath, and orange tubular flowers (see pp. 54 and 55).

SMITHIANTHA

A range of hybrids of this genus was grown and exhibited by Thomas Butcher Ltd of Croydon in the 1960s and they were well known as flowering pot plants for the greenhouse and conservatory under the name of temple bells. The scaly rhizomes are catkin-like, rather similar to large *Achimenes*, up to 2 in. (5 cm) long, and the plants multiply by forming several rhizomes under the soil as they die down after flowering (see p. 18). They will often, from a single rhizome, make an erect-stemmed plant up to 12 in. (30 cm) high, with 6 in. (15 cm), velvety, coloured leaves and a central pyramidal spike another 12 in. (30 cm) above this, consisting of tubular bell-shaped flowers in a range of colours from white through yellow, orange and red. The rhizomes need to be stored in a minimum temperature of 50°F (10°C) and they should be repotted and started into growth in July, one to a 5 in. (13 cm) pot using a peat-based compost. Water them with a high potash fertilizer at every watering once growth is well advanced, taking care not to let them get too dry in the early stages of growth. Keep in good light but not in direct sun, with a minimum temperature of 68°F (20°C), to flower in the late autumn.

Smithiantha cinnabarina. A stout 12 in. (30 cm)-stemmed plant with 6 in. (15 cm), broad, scalloped, velvety leaves, green covered with red hairs. The tubular, bell-shaped, red and yellow flowers are borne in a 10 in. (25 cm) pyramid from the top of the plant in late autumn, with up to 100 in a spike. Smaller spikes may sometimes be produced from the upper leaf axils as well.

S. zebrina. Similar to *S. cinnabarina* in size and habit, but the leaves are green with a deep purple suffusion, mainly along the veins. The yellow flowers are spotted with red in the throat.

Hybrids. Among the hybrids, S. 'Orange King' is one of the best known, having velvety purple-brown leaves and bright orange flowers (see also p. 23).

Opposite: *Smithiantha* hybrids have nodding foxglove-like flowers

Tuberous gesneriads

SINNINGIA

This genus contains the florist's gloxinia, the original species of which is *Sinningia speciosa*. This has now been hybridized and developed to an enormous extent, with a range of flower colours from white through red to deep purple, bicolor and spotted, some having giant trumpet flowers up to 5 in. (13 cm) across and with double-flowered forms also seen.

Dormant tubers are readily obtainable from most garden centres and bulb suppliers. These should be started into growth in spring in trays of moist moss peat or singly in 3½ in. (9 cm) pots of peat at a temperature of 70°F (21°C). Make sure the rounded side of the tuber is at the bottom and keep well shaded until the new growth appears from the top of the tuber. When a couple of pairs of leaves have developed, pot into a 5½ in. (14 cm) pot using a compost made up of equal volumes of moss peat and John Innes no. 2 compost. Grow on, watering only when the compost is dry each time and feeding with a high potash fertilizer at every other watering, and it will soon make a plant easily 12 in. (30 cm) across, with large, hairy, green leaves, often with lighter veins, borne on short stalks from a thick, hairy, upright stem. From the upper leaf axils, the large showy flowers are produced in numbers over a period of a few weeks, the season depending on when the tuber has been started into growth. Light but not sunny conditions will give the best results. When the production of flowers comes to an end, water should be gradually withheld and the foliage allowed to shrivel and dry until it is easily detached from the tuber. The tuber should then be stored dry, either in its pot or in a box of dry peat during the winter, at a minimum temperature of 50°F (10°C), to be restarted again the next year.

Apart from the large-flowered types with symmetrical-lobed wide-tubed flowers, there are the slipper-flowered forms with smaller, often curved tubes and with the lower lobes expanded to form a lip – almost like a streptocarpus flower. These are treated in the same way as the large-flowered hybrids. Both may be propagated by leaf cuttings (see p. 15).

Then we have the miniature sinningias, typified by S. 'Doll Baby'. They have S. *pusilla* and S. *concinna* in their parentage and these species impart an ever-blooming quality to their progeny.

Spotted flowers are just one of the variations to be found in the
Sinningia speciosa hybrids

The miniatures, if grown in an open-based compost and a temperature range of 68–77°F (20–25°C), with a high light intensity, shaded from direct sunlight, will flower twelve months of the year with a day length of 12 to 14 hours. The flowers are borne on upright wiry stems well above the 3 in. (7.5 cm) flat rosette of grey-green hairy leaves. The flowers usually have an open flat face with expanded lobes.

The miniatures all seem to set seed quite freely and the seed germinates well at a temperature of 70°F (21°C), to produce flowering plants in about six months (see p. 22). Like the florist's gloxinia, leaves can be rooted and will form a small tuber at the bottom of the cut stem to pot and grow on. In addition, when several stems are sent up from a tuber, as is often the case, some of these may be removed close to the tuber and will root readily in the summer months with hardly any break in flowering (see p. 21).

Named hybrids of the miniatures are not yet widely distributed, but seed of mixed colours is available from several leading seed suppliers.

Sinningia cardinalis. In cultivation for many years as *Gesneria cardinalis*, this makes a good-tempered houseplant flowering in

the summer. With the same treatment as for the florist's gloxinia, the light brown tuber will produce several stems up to about 10 in. (25 cm) high, with many 4 in. (10 cm), light green, hairy, rounded leaves. From the leaf axils, round buds are formed which develop into tubular, bright vermilion flowers, 2 in. (5 cm) long, hairy. The plant remains in flower for several months. It should be watered only when the compost is quite dry and should be fed with a high potash feed at every other watering while in flower.

S. leucotricha. Long known as *Rechsteineria leucotricha*, this forms an orange-coloured tuber up to 3 in. (7.5 cm) across, from which several stems usually develop to attain a height of about 8 in. (20 cm), with 6 in. (15 cm) leaves completely covered with long, silken, silver-white hairs. The thin-tubed flowers are ⅜ in. (1 cm) in diameter, soft pink, covered with white hairs. Like most of the members of the genus, it does not like too much water.

S. regina. This species from Brazil makes a tuber 2 in. (5 cm) across, which produces a short stem bearing up to ten hairy leaves 6 by 3 in. (15 × 7.5 cm), oval, with a scalloped edge, deep green with the veins lined with white. A flush of lilac-mauve slipper-shaped flowers is carried on erect stems well above the foliage for six weeks during the summer. It sets seed very freely.

Miniatures. S. 'Doll Baby' has lavender flowers with a whitish throat; S. 'Cindy' has purple and white flowers; and S. 'White Sprite', as the name suggests, is pure white.

A spectacular hybrid in the trial of florist's gloxinias at Wisley
Opposite: *Sinningia regina* is valuable both for its white-veined leaves and for its charming flowers

Further information

NURSERIES

Tony Clements' African Violet Centre, Station Road, Terrington St Clement, Kings Lynn, Norfolk PE34 4PL (*Saintpaulia, Streptocarpus*)

Efenechtyd Nurseries, Llanelidan, Ruthin, Clwyd, Wales LL15 2LG (*Streptocarpus, Columnea,* also other gesneriads)

Stanley Mossop, 36 Thorny Road, Thornhill, Egremont, Cumbria CA22 2RZ (*Achimenes, Smithiantha,* also *Gloxinia, Koehleria*)

K.J. Townsend, 17 Valerie Close, St Albans, Herts AL1 5JD (*Achimenes;* mail order only)

SOCIETIES

Saintpaulia and Houseplant Society, Miss N. Tanburn (Honorary Secretary), 82 Rossmore Court, Park Road, London NW1 6XY

American Gesneriad Society, PO Box 439 R, Beverly Farms, MA 01915, USA

BOOKS

The Miracle Houseplants – The Gesneriads, V.F. and G.A. Elbert (Crown Publishers, New York, 1976)

African Violets, Tony Clements (David and Charles, 1988)

Indoor Light Gardening Book, G.A. Elbert (Crown Publishers, New York, 1973)

Opposite: 'Banksii' is one of the older *Columnea* hybrids

Above: one of the modern *Streptocarpus* hybrids, with large broad-
lobed flowers
Below: a group of mixed *Saintpaulia* seedlings